Nature's Children

TROUT

John Woodward

GROLIER

FACTS IN BRIEF

Classification of Trout

Class: *Osteichthyes*

Order: *Salmoniformes* (salmonlike fish)

Family: *Salmonidae* (salmon and relatives)

Genus: *Salmo*

Species: Includes rainbow trout (*Oncorhynchus mykiss*), cutthroat trout (*O. clarki*), gila trout (*O. gilae)*, and golden trout (*O. aguabonita*).

World distribution.   In fresh water in North America and Europe and also in the Atlantic and eastern Pacific Oceans.

Habitat.   Streams, rivers, lakes, and mainly coastal seas.

Distinctive physical characteristics.   Sleek, round-bodied fish with scales on their bodies but not on their heads. Small, fleshy adipose fin on back in front of tail. Spotted, sometimes silvery.

Habits.   Mainly solitary.

Diet.   Small trout eat insects and small crustaceans such as freshwater shrimp. Bigger trout eat other fish.

© 2004 The Brown Reference Group plc
Printed and bound in U.S.A.
Edited by John Farndon and Angela Koo

Published by:

An imprint of Scholastic Library Publishing Old Sherman Turnpike, Danbury, Connecticut 06816

Library of Congress Cataloging-in-Publication Data
Woodward, John, 1954–
  Trout / John Woodward.
      p. cm. — (Nature's children)
  Includes index.
  Summary: Describes the physical characteristics, habits, and habitats of trout.
  ISBN 0–7172–5957–9 (set)   ISBN 0–7172–5976–5
  1. Trout—Juvenile literature. [1. Trout.] I. Title. II. Series.

QL638.S2W66 2004
597.5'7—dc21

2003049181

Contents

Trout are very tasty fish to eat. They are fun to catch, too, if you like fishing. Alive, they are beautiful, silvery fish that swim in rivers and streams that flow with clear, bright water called "trout streams."

At some time in their lives they may move into deeper, darker rivers and lakes. But they always make their way back to the bright trout streams to lay their eggs. The journey can be difficult, but the trout never give up unless the water has been polluted.

Some trout even swim out into the ocean. They change color and grow much bigger, and were once thought to be quite different fish. But basically they are just the same as the small trout that never leave their home streams. No one knows why some go to sea and some don't. So in some ways trout are still a bit of a mystery.

Opposite page: *If you're lucky, you may see trout leaping from the water as they swim upriver to lay their eggs.*

What Is a Trout?

If you saw a big silvery trout and a small Atlantic salmon side by side, you might have trouble telling them apart. That's because they are almost the same thing. They both belong to the same family of fish, the Salmonidae. It also includes some similar fish called chars, graylings, and whitefish. The American brook trout is actually a char, and it is sometimes called the brook char.

There are at least five species of trout. The rainbow trout, cutthroat trout, gila trout, and golden trout are all native Americans. The brown trout is European. But the rainbow and brown trout have been introduced all over the world, and both species now live in both America and Europe. Confusingly, they also have different names depending on where they live and how they look.

Trout have streamlined, muscular bodies—ideal for swimming upstream against strong currents.

Rainbows, Silver, and Gold

The most widespread American trout is the rainbow, which gets its name from the pinkish, iridescent "rainbow" stripe along each flank. But just to make things difficult, not all rainbow trout have rainbow stripes. The big ones that live in large lakes are silvery instead and are called kamloops. There is also a silvery type that lives in the ocean for part of its life. You'll read about it later.

The rainbow trout has a close relative called the cutthroat trout, which is named for the red mark beneath its head. It lives in similar places, in the rivers to the west of the Rocky Mountains. The much rarer golden trout lives naturally in a few streams and lakes in the California Sierra Mountains. The very rare gila trout is found only in New Mexico.

Opposite page:
You can usually identify an adult rainbow trout by the reddish-pink "rainbow" band down its side.

Spotty Brownies

The trout that live wild in Europe are brown trout. Typical "brownies" have dark backs, yellowish bellies, and spotted, silvery sides, but they vary a lot. There are big silver lake trout and small spotted stream trout. The ones that live in clear, bright water are paler than those that live in brown-stained rivers. The paler ones often have quite small dark spots, while the darker ones usually have bigger spots. The spots are sometimes surrounded by pale rings. Many have rusty red spots as well, especially during the breeding season.

All these variations mean that two brown trout can look like completely different fish. In some places different forms live in the same water, but they seem to avoid breeding with each other. Lough Melvin in Ireland has five different forms, and scientists have figured out that they have lived together in the same lake for at least 5,000 years.

Steelheads and Sea Trout

Some rainbow trout and brown trout spend part of their lives at sea. There is a lot more food for them there, so they eat more and grow much bigger than normal. They are also more silvery than the ones that live in fresh water. That gives them better camouflage in the ocean. Rainbow trout that live at sea are called steelheads. Sea-going brown trout are called sea trout.

Moving from fresh water to salt water is difficult for a fish. But the extra food in the ocean makes it worthwhile, especially in places like California. Here the rivers run very low in summer, so the local rainbow trout head out into the Pacific Ocean. The habit of venturing out to sea runs in families. When Californian rainbow trout eggs were put in European rivers, the fish that hatched turned out to be the sea-going kind. They soon disappeared out into the Atlantic.

Leaping Salmon

The most famous relatives of trout are the salmon. They include the Atlantic salmon and five different species of Pacific salmon. They are all big, powerful fish that spend most of their lives feeding at sea on smaller fish. When they are ready to spawn, they swim up rivers to reach shallow fresh waters. A Chinook salmon may travel over 2,400 miles (3,860 kilometers) up the Yukon River in Alaska to reach its spawning site. On the way salmon of all kinds often perform astounding leaps from the water to get through waterfalls and rapids.

Atlantic salmon may make this journey several times. Pacific salmon make it just once, because they are so exhausted after spawning that they die. They do not go to waste, though, because the dead and dying salmon are a favorite food of grizzly bears and bald eagles.

Opposite page:
To get back to their spawning grounds far upriver, Atlantic salmon may have to make fantastic leaps up waterfalls.

Shape and Size

Opposite page:
In big rivers trout find lots of food. That means they can grow huge, like the trout caught by this fisher.

Like all the fish in the salmon family, a trout has a small, fleshy adipose fin on its back between its main dorsal fin and its tail. It has small scales all over its body, except on its head, and its skin is also protected by a layer of slime. It is sleek and streamlined, with a powerful tail fin to drive it through the water. A pair of pectoral fins just behind its head helps it maneuver at low speed.

A trout's size depends on how much it eats. There is not much food in small streams, so many stream trout only reach about 10 inches (25 centimeters) long. They can grow to about 39 inches (100 centimeters) in bigger rivers and lakes. But the biggest trout are the ones that feed on other fish at sea. They can reach 55 inches (140 centimeters) and weigh over 35 pounds (16 kilograms).

Inside a Trout

Most of a trout's body is made up of big blocks of muscle. They are pale brown or even pink. They lie along each side of a strong but flexible backbone. It is made of a chain of small bones called vertebrae. Attached to them are a lot of long, thin bones that support the trout's body.

All the trout's vital organs lie in a cavity below its backbone. They include its heart, liver, and intestine, as well as a long balloonlike structure called the swim bladder. It is filled with gas and works as a float. By altering the amount of gas in its swim bladder, the trout can rise and fall in the water just like a submarine.

The trout's skull is quite complicated, with a special bony place for its brain and various bones to support its eyes, jaws, and gills.

Opposite page: *These are the bones of a trout. You can see the strong, flexible backbone down the middle. You can also see all the side bones that support the trout's body.*

Nonstop Swimming

Like most fish, a trout swims by flexing its body and tail fin in a wavy S-shape. That pushes water toward its tail, forcing the trout forward. The trout is so beautifully streamlined that the slightest twitch makes it glide through the water. Its body fins help push it along, keep it steady, and steer. It can also row itself along using its pectoral fins. This method is slow but very precise, allowing the fish to maneuver into tight spots and even swim backward.

The trout uses its big, pale muscles for fast swimming when it wants to get out of trouble. When it is moving slowly, it uses a much thinner layer of dark brown muscle. This type of muscle is not very powerful, but it never gets tired. It allows the fish to keep swimming forever against a steady current.

A trout is perfectly built for swimming, with a big tail for driving it along and body fins to steer with.

The semicircles on the side of the trout's head are the tough flaps that cover its gills.

Breathing Underwater

All animals need a gas called oxygen to turn their food into energy. Oxygen is part of the air, so land animals can get what they need by breathing. But there is oxygen in water too—especially the cool, clear water favored by trout. So a fish needs a way of drawing that oxygen into its body.

It does so using very delicate, feathery structures called gills, which are protected by tough gill covers. The gills are bright red because they are basically transparent tubes filled with blood. As the fish swims along, water flows in through its mouth and out through the gill covers, passing over the gills. The oxygen in the water seeps through the thin walls of the gills and into the fish's blood. Meanwhile a waste gas called carbon dioxide seeps out and is carried away.

Senses

A trout finds its way around by sight, scent, and feel. It cannot see far, but that's because the water makes everything in the distance invisible. A trout can spot prey up to 50 feet (15 meters) away in clear water, which is more than many fish can manage.

Its sense of smell is very good. Since scent carries well in water, a trout can sniff its way toward a meal from far away. Trout that venture out into the ocean find their way home by scenting the water of their home rivers.

A trout also has an acute sense of feel. It can detect tiny changes in water pressure through special touch organs along its flanks. So it can feel when another fish swims by in the dark, or when it is near a big obstacle such as a rock.

Like most fish that hunt, trout have very sharp eyes for spotting prey.

Where Do Trout Live?

Some fish can live in muddy and even smelly water, but not trout. They need clear water with no pollution. They also like it quite cool, because cool water contains more oxygen. So clear upland streams are better places for trout than big muddy rivers. They always breed in clear, cool water.

Despite being fussy about water quality, they are quite happy to move from rivers to the sea and back again. That causes problems for most fish, which live in either fresh water or salt water but not both. Trout seem able to make the switch without trouble, as long as they take their time. So, many trout that hatch near the sea swim out into the ocean when they get big enough. They do not go far, though. They usually stay near the coast, and after two or three years they come back to their home rivers to spawn.

Opposite page: *Trout are very particular about where they live. Many like to live in cool, clear upland streams like this.*

What Do Trout Eat?

Opposite page:
This picture is entirely faked, but it could happen. Sometimes, trout do leap from the water to catch flying insects.

The small trout that live in streams and small rivers eat animals like freshwater shrimp and insects. They particularly like flying insects such as mayflies that crash-land in the water after breeding. Adult mayflies live for only a few hours, and many end up in the bellies of hungry trout.

Bigger trout that live in lakes eat small fish as well. Some will even eat young trout, which could be their own kids! Fish have a lot more food value than insects, so the more the trout eat, the bigger they get.

The biggest trout of all live in the ocean. Here they enjoy a rich diet of fish like sprats and capelin. They eat other animals too, and trout that have been eating shrimps and crabs at sea have pale pink flesh, rather like salmon.

Hunting

River trout spend a lot of their time in deep pools or hidden in holes under a river bank. But when they are hungry, they come out and hunt in shallower water. They often "hang" in the current, swimming against the river flow so they stay in the same place. As the water flows past, it carries small animals with it. The trout watch for them and slip from side to side to snap them up.

The trout that live in lakes like to hunt in the shallow water near the edge. They often come to the surface in the evening to snatch flies that have landed on the water, sometimes with a loud "plop"! But bigger trout that eat other fish generally stay in deep water where they can ambush their victims in the gloom.

Streams carry small creatures along with them. So trout don't always need to swim after them. They just hang in the water and wait for their food to be swept by.

Migration

When trout are ready to breed, they have to find a stretch of water that gives their eggs and young the best chance of survival. The easiest way of doing this is to return to the place where they were born themselves.

Every trout can remember the scent of its home water, and it has an instinct to swim toward it when it is time to breed. The journey may not take long for a small river trout. But bigger ones that have found their way to lakes or the ocean often have to travel for many days. They may have to swim up rapids and even jump waterfalls like salmon, so they often rest in quiet pools for a while before going on. Eventually they reach the end of this special journey, or migration, and get ready to spawn (have kids).

A female trout scoops out a hollow in the riverbed to lay its eggs in by thrashing its body.

Spawning

As the female and male trout swim toward their spawning grounds, their eggs and sperm develop inside their bodies. The fish become more colorful, and brown trout get red spots. And by the time they reach the end of their journey, the males have developed strangely hooked lower jaws.

Their goal is a stretch of shallow, clear river running over clean gravel. When a female finds the right spot, she digs a hollow with her tail, then lays up to 1,500 orange eggs, each a quarter-inch (6 millimeters) across. The male then takes her place and spreads sperm over the eggs to fertilize them. They cover the eggs with gravel to keep them from being swept away by the current. After spawning, the fish drift away and may die, but many survive to spawn again in other years.

Opposite page: *These one-day-old brown trout eggs should really be covered in gravel to save them from being washed away by the stream current.*

Hatching

Trout eggs stay hidden in the gravel for at least six weeks before hatching. If the water is very cold, they develop more slowly and may take up to eight weeks to hatch. The tiny fish ("fry") that emerge have bags full of egg yolk attached to their stomachs. The yolk provides all the food they need for another three weeks, or up to six weeks in cold water. They can hide in the gravel out of sight of other fish that might eat them.

When they run out of yolk, the trout fry start eating very small stream animals, such as the tiniest shrimp and water fleas. That gives the baby fish practice in locating and catching prey, as well as vital food.

Baby trout begin to hatch after six to eight weeks. Here you can see the dark eye of one emerging from its shell.

When young, brown trout are called parr and have distinctive dark "thumb prints" down the side.

Growing Up

When they start looking for their own food, baby trout don't look like trout at all. They are only about an inch (25 millimeters) long, with thin, ribbonlike bodies. But as they grow, they start looking more like their parents. Young brown trout become spotted and silvery, with many red spots. They also have dark marks on their sides that look rather like thumb prints. These young, "thumb-printed" fish are called parr.

As they grow, they eat bigger prey, eventually taking large insects like mayflies. If there is plenty of food, they may have grown to about 6 inches (15 centimeters) long by the end of their first summer. If there is less food, they grow much more slowly. Trout that stay in rivers where there are only insects to eat stay small all their lives. The ones that feed on fish grow much faster and get much bigger.

Deadly Enemies

Opposite page:
For a trout danger can strike from out of the water as well as in it. Many trout are caught like this—by a heron darting its sharp beak into the water.

Young trout are eaten by all kinds of animals, including bigger trout. As they get bigger, they become more difficult to catch, but many animals still try. In rivers medium-sized trout are eaten by big killer fish called pike and seized by herons, otters, and even bears. The biggest lake fish probably do not have any enemies except people.

Out in the ocean steelheads and sea trout have to avoid big hunters like tuna, marlin, and sharks. They are also caught by seals and sea lions. But some of their most deadly enemies are killer whales. These huge ocean hunters corral fish by swimming around them and forcing them to bunch together in tight shoals. The killer whales then plow into the shoals and eat as many as they can.

Trout Fishing

People have been catching and eating trout for thousands of years. They catch them with nets, traps, and baited hooks, but the most common way of catching a trout is fly fishing.

The "fly" is a hook with a bunch of small feathers tied to it. To the trout it looks like something it might like to eat. A "dry fly" floats on the surface of the water, drifting on the current like a dying mayfly. Anglers (fishermen) often use it to catch rainbow and brown trout in rivers and streams. A "wet fly" sinks and imitates a small fish. It often works better with big steelheads and sea trout.

Another way of catching a trout hiding under a river bank is to "tickle" it. An expert carefully feels beneath the trout and strokes its belly. As it drifts into a dream, the "tickler" flips it out onto the bank.

Opposite page: Many fishers like catching trout both for sport and to eat. They lure the fish by tying feathers to the hook so that it looks like a tasty insect.

Trout Farming

Trout are such important food fish that huge numbers are raised specially for eating on "trout farms." The usual type raised on a trout farm is the rainbow trout, but brown trout and even golden trout are farmed too.

The farm is really a series of pools full of water that is always being pumped through filters to keep it clean. The fish are fed with special food that is rather like the shrimp eaten by sea trout and steelheads. It turns their flesh pink in the same way and makes it look better to eat.

Many people think that farmed trout do not taste as good as wild trout. But if all the trout that we eat were taken from rivers and seas, there might be none left. So trout farming probably helps stop wild trout from being wiped out by overfishing.

Pollution and Conservation

The biggest problem for wild trout is pollution. They like water that is clean, cool, and rich in oxygen. And anything that changes that can make them disappear. It might be poisonous chemicals from factories or pesticides sprayed on farmland. But sewage or fertilizer can be just as bad, because they make tiny animals (microbes) grow in the water that use up all the oxygen.

The trout that stay in small streams may never suffer from pollution. But the bigger ones that swim out to sea have to swim along big rivers that may be polluted by cities, industries, or farming. If they don't like the water, they turn back or may even die. So sea trout are most common in wilder regions where the big rivers flowing down to the ocean are still clear and bright.

Words to Know

Adipose fin The small, fleshy fin on the back of a trout or salmon near its tail.

Dorsal fin The fin in the center of a fish's back.

Fry Newly hatched baby fish.

Gills Organs that absorb oxygen from water and get rid of waste carbon dioxide.

Iridescent Glittering with rainbow colors.

Kamloops A big rainbow trout that lives in a lake.

Migration A long journey to find food or to breed.

Pectoral fins The paired fins near a fish's head.

Spawning A type of breeding in which the female lays eggs, and the male spreads sperm on them afterward.

Species A particular type of animal. A tiger, for example, is a species of cat.

Sperm The male cells that fuse with eggs to make them grow into young animals.

Steelhead A rainbow trout that goes to sea.

Vertebrae The bones that link together in a chain to form an animal's backbone.

Yolk The food that keeps a baby animal alive inside an egg and sometimes after it hatches.

INDEX

Cover Photo: NHPA: Jeff Goodman
Photo Credits: Ardea: 17, Martin W. Grosnick 18, Chris Knights 41, Ken Lucas 22, P.&J. Morrin 33; Bruce Coleman: Jane Burton 37, Kevin Cullimore 42, Andrew Purcell 25, Kim Taylor 8, 29; NHPA: Agence Nature 38, B.&C. Alexander 14, Lutra 21; Oxford Scientific Films: 30, Alan & Sandy Carey 26, Okapia 4, Hans Reinhard 12/13, Science Pictures Ltd. 34; Still Pictures: Mike Jackson 45, Norbert Wu 7.